CATHOLIC CHARISMATIC RENEWAL AND LIFE IN THE SPIRIT

MICHAEL ATTAH ONUH
Understanding the Holy Spirit, His Gifts, the Pentecost Experience and the Building of an Ever-Deepening Relationship with Him.

COPY RIGHT

Catholic Charismatic Renewal and Life in the Spirit

Michael Attah Onuh

Nihil Obstat: The Reverend Marcus Holden MA (Oxon), S.T.L

IMPRIMATUR: The Reverend Monsignor Matthew J Dickens VG

19th June 2018

ABOUT THE AUTHOR

The author of this book "CATHOLIC CHARISMATIC RENEWAL AND LIFE IN THE SPIRIT", Michael Attah Onuh, hails from Okpoga Local Government Area of Benue State. He is happily married with children and grand-children and currently resides in London with his beloved wife, Mrs Catherine Enuwa Onuh.

Michael has been a member of, and or a leader of different fellowships and prayer groups, at various times including being a member of Catholic Charismatic Renewal at St. Augustine's Catholic Church, Congo, Institute of Administration, Zaria, Nigeria; Leader of Bible Study Society, St. Anthony's Catholic Church, Lagos and a member of the Westminster Cathedral Catholic Charismatic Renewal, London.

The author was an Assistant Chaplain at Croydon College, in charge of Morning Prayers for both staff and students, and the sharing of Bible studies with the students of the Christian Union. He is one of the leaders of Christ the King Catholic Charismatic Renewal, Thornton Heath, Croydon, South London. Furthermore, Michael is currently the General Co-ordinator of the Catholic Charismatic Renewal, Good Shepherd Catholic Church, New Addington, Croydon. The author has the following academic qualifications of which many are religion related: Diploma in Insurance, Ahmadu Bello University, Zaria, Nigeria; Associate Chartered Insurance Institute, (ACII), UK; Diploma in Pastoral Theology, EPS, (Education for Parish Service) London; BA (Hons) Theology for Ministry, Middlesex University, UK; Postgraduate Certificate in Ecumenical Chaplaincy, Ushaw

College, Durham, UK; Postgraduate Certificate in Education, (PGCE) Maryvale Birmingham, UK and Post graduate Diploma in Religious Education (RE), Warwick University, UK.

ABOUT THE BOOK

The book, "Catholic Charismatic Renewal and Life in the Spirit" is a must read for all Christians who desire the deeper understanding of the Holy Spirit and the Pentecostal experience. It is a book that will help one to understand the work of the third Person of the Blessed Trinity, God the Holy Spirit and to maintain an ever-deepening relationship with Him. It illuminatingly explains gifts, in particular the gifts of prophecy and tongues which the author depicted as the prominent gifts of Pentecost. He maintains that the Fresh Outpouring of Pentecost is a continuous event and explains the purpose of sending the Holy Spirit.

The author argues that the gift of tongues is for every baptised Christian but not mandatory, and he elaborately explains the spiritual benefits of the gift of tongues, as well as how to desire the gift of tongues and indeed other gifts. The evidence of the author's knowledge of the bible was amazing as he underpins all his claims with precise quotations from the Holy Book. This book is timely because it is only through the work of the Spirit that the tide of our contemporary society, in which shameful sins are increasingly being applauded, supported and even legally enthroned, will be turned. The understanding of the renewal leads to life in the Spirit which this book aims to foster. I therefore encourage you not only to get this book, but also to read it for the all-important understanding and to deepen relationship with God.

Paulinus Nwosu
The author of 'Church for the Faithful'

TABLE OF CONTENTS

DEDICATION AND ACKNOWLEDGEMENT

This book is dedicated to the Holy Spirit for the great inspirations I received from Him in writing this book. Our ability to worship God, live the Gospel, and have a personal relationship with Jesus, as our personal Lord and Saviour, depends on the Holy Spirit's empowerments and revelation to us as believers.

With profound thanks I express my gratefulness to God our Father in heaven, the Father of our Lord and Saviour Jesus Christ, the Light of the nations. To Him alone be the glory (Isaiah 42:8) for the necessary assistance I received in writing this book. My gratitude also goes to the Holy Spirit the Paraclete for the great inspiration accorded me by Him.

I am also greatly indebted to my mentor Mr Paulinus C. Nwosu, the Evangelical Ministry Leader of Christ the King Catholic Charismatic Renewal, St. Andrew's Catholic Church, Thornton Heath, for helping to improve my written skills, primarily for my first book "Strong Reasons Why Jesus is the Only Way to Salvation" (yet to be published) and for this book "Catholic Charismatic Renewal and Life in the Spirit". He did not only critically read the book, but also played a remarkable role in the editing of the book.

Furthermore, my appreciation goes to my beloved wife, Mrs Catherine Enuwa Onuh for her patience which engendered an atmosphere conducive for writing. I am also indebted to my son, Matthew Attah Onuh who, actually worked hard to find a publisher within the short period that I was looking for a publisher.

Finally, I wish to express my heartfelt gratitude to my parish priest, Rev. Fr. Con Boyle, for proofreading the book.

Michael Attah Onuh 17th June 2015

"Catholic Charismatic Renewal and Life in the Spirit" (Michael Attah Onuh)

Foreword

In this publication Michael Attah Onuh sets out a summary of the Movement known as the Catholic Charismatic Renewal.

He is very active in the parish of The Good Shepherd Roman Catholic Church, New Addington, Croydon, Surrey, England. He has set up a weekly Charismatic prayer meeting, and is equally active in traditional worship in the parish.

In this written work he demonstrates that the Catholic Charismatic Renewal is at the heart of the Church, and fully obedient to the Magisterium.

Central to his thought is the absolute centrality of Baptism. Through this primary and wondrous sacrament we are "born again". (On our date of birth we were born into earthly life; on our day of Baptism we were born into God's family).

The baptizing by John the Baptist was merely a water baptism unto repentance for sin, as the Baptist himself assured us. Only Jesus Christ, being truly God, could bring the Baptism of the Spirit. Only God could bring or bestow God.

Therefore the Catholic Charismatic Renewal is the work of the Holy Spirit. Jesus himself assured us: "My Father and I are always working". This is the working of the Holy Spirit, who is that great mutual love between God the Father and God the Son.

May all of you who read Michael's publication be nourished in mind, heart, body and soul. May you journey, in great confidence, towards that personal call: "Come, blessed of my Father."

Fr. Con Boyle (parish priest) – Good Shepherd RC church
23rd April 2015

Introduction

In Christianity (the life of Christians), there are many challenges because it is a call to holiness. After Christian Baptism one is born of God (Jn 3:4-5; 1 Jn 5:4-5). This is a new spiritual rebirth into God's family, as citizens of heaven. Divine grace and forgiveness of sin allow a personal relationship with God through Jesus Christ the only begotten Son of God. A personal relationship with God means that he or she is able to commune with God, that is, to have fellowship with Him **(Rev.3:20).** The Holy Spirit is the agent of the sacramental baptism. Our relationship with God can be broken through serious sins and renewed through repentance – hence the idea of **Renewal.**

This book explains that **Renewal** is about the new life in Christ, **"baptism in the Holy Spirit".** It is about the promise of Jesus Christ to baptize Christians with the Holy Spirit and fire **(Mt 3:11; Lk 3:16; Mk 1: 8; Jn 1:33; Acts 1:5; Acts 11:16 and Eph 5:18).** These texts are not about the renewal in the Holy Spirit only but also refer to sacramental baptism. **The "baptism in the Spirit"** is a Pentecost phenomenon, i.e, the activities of the Holy Spirit, His gifts, empowerments or enablements to Christians. One can see the importance of the **"baptism in the Holy Spirit"** from the fact that all the evangelists and other sacred Scriptures carry it.

The author is of the view that just as it is possible to have personal relationship with God the Father, it is possible to have a personal relationship with the Holy Spirit. He is a Person, the

Third Person of the Blessed Trinity, and He is buttressed with the following extract from JESUS:

"I will not leave you orphans; I will come to you. But the Helper, the Holy Spirit, whom the Father will send in my name, He will teach you all things, and bring to your remembrance all that I said to you" (Jn 14:18; Jn 14:26).

In this book, the author takes time to explain the main gifts of the Holy Spirit featured at Pentecost – the gift of Prophecy and the gift of Tongues. St. Paul says that these two gifts are about love **(1 Cor 14:1).** Also discussed and deeply explained are other traditional gifts and the symbols of the Holy Spirit and intrinsically how to desire, seek, receive and use the gifts to the glory of God.

The book will benefit any Christian and even non-Christians who desire deeper knowledge of God and closer relationship with God by the power of the Holy Spirit. May God bless you even as He further reveals Himself to you through this book.

Michael Attah Onuh
17th June 2015, London

CATHOLIC CHARISMATIC RENEWAL AND

LIFE IN THE SPIRIT

CHAPTER ONE

The Catholic Charismatic Renewal is a Catholic spirituality. Sometimes it is called a "Movement". It is a movement within the Catholic Church. It is not a church on its own. It is a part of the Catholic Church, living every doctrine and the sacramental life of the Catholic Church. It is called a **"Renewal"** because it helps to transform and regenerate the spiritual lives of believers **(Rom 12: 1-2; Titus 3:5).**

It has the support of Popes, for example:
The Catholic Charismatic Renewal is an answered prayer of **Pope John XXIII,** "Renew your wonders in our time, as though for a new Pentecost". This prayer was made on 25th December 1961 during his convocation of Vatican II Council.

Pope John Paul II called the emergence of the Renewal a "gift of the Holy Spirit to the Church" (March 14, 1992). On the eve of Pentecost 2004 he stated, "Thanks to the Charismatic Movement, a multitude of Christians, men and women, young people and adults, have rediscovered Pentecost as a living reality in their daily lives. I hope that the spirituality of Pentecost will spread in the Church as a renewed incentive to prayer, holiness, communion and proclamation".

"Pope Francis discovers the Charismatic Movement as a gift to the whole Church"

By France X. Rocca Catholic News Service, Vatican Letter
August 9th 2014.

Further references about the Pope from the Vatican Letter are worth considering:

> **"I don't think that the charismatic renewal merely prevents people from passing over to Pentecostal denominations," Pope Francis said. "No! It is also a service to the Church herself! It renews us".**

"The movements are necessary, the movements are a grace of the Spirit," the Pope added, speaking of ecclesial movements in general. Everyone seeks his own movement, according to his own charism, where the Holy Spirit draws him or her.

The Renewal is about **"baptism in the Spirit".** [1] It is about the promise of Jesus Christ to baptize Christians with the Holy Spirit and fire. It is a Charismatic gift (a Pentecostal phenomenon). Biblical references can make things clear here:

> **"While staying with them, He ordered them not to leave Jerusalem, but to wait there for the promise of the Father 'This', He said, 'is what you have heard from me; for John baptized with water, but you will be baptized with the Holy Spirit not many days from now". This**

experience of baptism in the Spirit or being bathed in the Spirit is also linked to sacramental Confirmation. The Church links together the grace of Pentecost and the renewal gifts in Confirmation (Acts 1:4-5; Acts 11:16

"I baptize you with water for repentance, but one who is more powerful than I is coming after me: I am not worthy to carry His sandals. He will baptize you with the Holy Spirit and fire" [2] (Mt 3:11; Lk 3:16; 1:8; Jn 1:33).

---

1 This is a renewal of the gifts the Holy Spirit bestows on us in our sacramental baptism.
2 This baptism is principally sacramental baptism but can also refer secondarily to the gifts and charisms (boldness and enablements) brought to the lives of Christians by renewal in the Holy Spirit.

Reflection

The **"baptism in the Holy Spirit"** is a Pentecostal phenomenon (Charismatic gifts), that is, the activities of the Holy Spirit, His gifts, empowerments or enablement to Christians. Baptism in the Holy Spirit may refer in part to growth in sanctifying grace, to gifts that flow from the life of grace and even to confirmation. Some people believe that it is the equivalent of the sacrament of Confirmation. It is about the marvellous strength of the Holy Spirit and fire to the Apostles at Pentecost.

This marvellous strength of the Holy Spirit wiped away their fears, gave them boldness, and allowed the Church to be established on a sound foundation - Jesus Christ.

Jesus refers to this marvellous strength of the Holy Spirit and fire as **"the promise of the Father"**. It is a permanent gift to the Church. One can see the importance of the **"baptism of the Holy Spirit"** from the fact that all the evangelists and other sacred Scriptures carry it. In the Catholic tradition there are different interpretations.

Definition of Baptism

The most comprehensive definition of Baptism is from the Catechism of the Catholic Church (CCC 683):

> **"Baptism gives us the grace of new birth in God the Father, through his Son, in the Holy Spirit. For those who bear God's Spirit are led to the Word, that is, to the Son and the Son presents them to the Father, and the Father confers incorruptibility on them. And it is impossible to see God's Son without the Spirit, and no one can approach the Father without the Son, for the knowledge of the Father is the Son, and the knowledge of God's Son is obtained through the Holy Spirit" (Catechism of the Catholic Church CCC 683 p.157).**

Reflection

This definition is a complete message of eternal life – the grace of new birth in the Father, through the Son, and in the Holy Spirit. The Father confers incorruptibility on us –

eternity and the gift of the Holy Spirit. Without the Holy Spirit no one can know the Father and the Son **(1 Cor 12:3).** Jesus affirms the phrase **"and no one can approach the Father without the Son"** by saying:

> **"Everything has been entrusted to me by my Father; and no one knows the Son   except the Father; just as no one knows the Father except the Son and those to whom the Son chooses to reveal Him" (Mt 11:27).**

We gather from the above Biblical reference from Matthew's Gospel that we know the Father as Christians because Jesus has revealed Him to us. This definition is self-explanatory. It shows the Blessed Trinity in action and the salvific plan of God being led by the Holy Spirit. So, we can see from this definition, the essence of Christian Baptism.

Baptism unto repentance and baptism in the Holy Spirit
The Gospel of Matthew refers to both **"Baptism unto repentance"** and **"baptism in the Spirit".** This can be seen as quoted below:

> **"I baptise you in water for repentance, but the one who follows me is more powerful than I am, and I am not fit to carry his sandals; he will baptise you with the Holy Spirit and fire" (Mt 3:11).**

According to the interpretation of the tradition of the Catholic Church, this does not mean that there are two baptisms. This is because to regard it as two baptisms would confuse people as we can see from a quotation from Rev. Fr. Benedict M. Heron below:

> **"Some Catholics prefer to use the expression 'Release of the Spirit' to avoid any possible confusion with the sacrament of Baptism. (In French they speak of l'effusion de Spirit, and in Italian l'effusione dello Spirito)" (Benedict M. Heron, 1992:9 "The Catholic Charismatic Renewal")**

Rev. Fr. Benedict M. Heron has so many years' standing of Catholic Charismatic Renewal experience.
The original Baptism (Baptism unto repentance) gives rise to **"baptism in the Holy Spirit"**.

> **Rev. Fr. Marcus Holden, describes "baptism in the Holy Spirit" "as growth in the grace given in Baptism". It is part of what is traditionally described in spiritual theology as 'growth in sanctifying grace'. It is not in any strict theological sense a 'new Baptism' but rather a development in being a child of God in Christ".**

Sanctifying Grace

Sanctifying grace is the restoration of the image of God that we lost through Original Sin. Jesus restored our impaired

21

image of God by His sacrificial or redemptive work of salvation on the cross. The likeness of God is the nature of God, His holiness and Spirit, which He imparted to humanity through Adam.

Rev. Fr. Dom Wulstan Mork, O.S.B. describes sanctifying grace as follows:

> **"What else is this grace but the elevation of man to God's life, to a plane of living supernatural to man, so that he can know and love God as God knows and loves Himself"** **(Dom W.M. 2004:8)**

The term **"sanctifying grace"** is not in the Bible. However, two Biblical texts from St. Paul's First Letter to Corinthians can shed light on it:

> **"He is the source of your life in Christ Jesus, who become for us wisdom from God, and righteousness and sanctification and redemption, in order that, as it is written, "Let the one who boasts, boast in the Lord" (1 Cor 1:30-31).**

> **"And this is what some of you used to be. But you were washed, you were sanctified, you were justified in the name of the Lord Jesus Christ and in the Spirit of our God" (1 Cor 6:11).**

Reflection

Judging from the two Biblical references above from St. Paul, one can say that **"sanctifying grace"** is life in Christ. Life in Christ is life in the Spirit **(pneuma).** Life in the Spirit is life in the supernatural. Life in the supernatural is life above the natural which is flesh **(sarx)** – the sinful nature.

St. Paul describes the life in Christ or supernatural life as putting off the **"old man"** and putting on the **"new man" (Eph 4:22-24).** **"Old man"** metaphorically means our former life of sin before our repentance. Our life in Christ is new life – life in the Spirit.

Another function of sanctifying grace

There is a variation in the way sanctifying grace works. Other virtues we receive as part of sanctifying grace are: wisdom, righteousness and justification. We can cease to be wise and we can lose our state of grace, or righteousness, by serious sin. St. Paul says, "We work out our salvation in fear and trembling" **(Phil 2:12).** Sanctification is a continuous process in our journey to the Kingdom of God. Whenever we fall into sin, we break relationship with the Father. We get up again after we have been to the Sacrament of Healing (Reconciliation or Penance). The Father gives us again sanctifying grace and we also receive actual grace. Then we come back to our state of grace again fully.

Actual grace

Actual grace helps to keep sanctifying grace alive in the soul. Sanctifying grace is the supernatural life of God in the soul – the likeness of God in the soul. We can receive sanctifying grace from baptism and also Sacrament of Reconciliation. It can increase as well as decrease within us. Actual graces too can increase and decrease. Actual grace is given throughout our lives. We are saved by actual grace from sin.

Definition of **"Actual grace"** by "The Essential Catholic Survival Guide" will make it very clear:

"Actual grace, by contrast, is a supernatural push or encouragement. It's transient. It doesn't live in the soul but acts from outside, so to speak. It is a supernatural kick in the pants. It gets the will and the intellect moving so we can seek and keep sanctifying grace"

(The Essential Catholic Survival Guide San Diego: 2005, Catholic Answers to Tough Questions About Faith, p.222)

Grace is gratuitous: That is to say that our salvation is a free gift of God. St. Paul makes it quite clear by saying:

"For by grace you have been saved through faith, and this is not your own doing; it is the gift of God – not the result of works, so that no one may boast. For we are what he has made us, created in Christ Jesus for good works, which God prepared beforehand to be our way of life"
(Eph 2:8-10).

24

We are expected to be in a state of grace always. This is not humanly possible because of our tendency to fall into sin, called **"concupiscence" (strong passion)**. For this reason it is the will of God to sanctify us again and again after a fall – a broken relationship with God. This makes sanctifying grace a continuous process!

A Biblical reference below will support my claim above:
> **"For this is the will of God, even your sanctification, that you abstain from fornication; that each one of you knows how to control your own body in holiness and honour, not with lustful passion"(1 Thes 4:3-5).**

Baptism unto repentance (John's Baptism)
Baptism unto repentance takes away the guilt of Original Sin. John's baptism is not sacramental baptism like the one instituted by Jesus Christ. Sacramental baptism is the baptism done in the name of Jesus Christ. This can be made clear by Peter's preaching on the Pentecost day, "Repent, and be baptized every one of you in the name of Jesus Christ for the forgiveness of your sins; and you shall receive the gift of the Holy Spirit" (CCC 1226; Acts 2:38). It also enables us to commune with God through Jesus Christ by grace.

Thereafter "baptism in the Holy Spirit" empowers a believer for ministry in the Church, for a deepening of a relationship with God through Jesus Christ, and to go out boldly on evangelization.

One can evangelize with the way one lives and conducts his or her affairs. Evangelization is not confined to going out only.

The next stage is to be filled with the words of Jesus, declared for us on the pages of the Bible. This is what He means when He says:

> " Those who love Me will keep My word, and my Father will love them, and we will come and make our home with them; You have already been cleansed by the word that I have spoken to you; If you abide in Me, and my words abide in you, ask whatever you wish and it will be done for you" (Jn 14:23; Jn 15:3; and Jn 15:7).

The Holy Spirit is given to a believer after baptism and he/she becomes a **new creation,** a citizen of heaven, capable of a relationship with God through Jesus Christ by grace. This is the stage when a believer is having Jesus as his or her **Personal Lord and Saviour,** and the life of personal transformation and regeneration begins **(Rom 12:2; and Titus 3:5).** This is what St. Paul refers to as **"a new creation"** – So if anyone is in Christ, there is a new creation: everything old has passed away; see everything has become new! **(2 Cor 5:17).** It is described in Titus as **"the water of rebirth and renewal by the Holy Spirit"** (Titus 3:5).

New Birth (New Life in Christ)

New birth means a new being and a changed way of life. This changed way of life is made possible through sacramental baptism which makes one a new creation. It is not that a person is changed into another person entirely. No. It is not a changed personality. A person remains a unique person as created by God. Nicodemus, a Jewish teacher, asked Jesus whether a person could enter into his mother's womb a second time and be born again **(Jn 3:4)**. Jesus said **"No"**. A new birth gives a person a new relationship with God and neighbour. It is a spiritual rebirth – freedom from the dominion of sin to the freedom of Christ. This is when one lives for Christ by not gratifying the deeds of the flesh **(Gal 5:16)**.

One old time Chorus comes to mind here:

> **"Things I used to do, I do them no more; there is**
> **a great change since I became born again".**

I will come back to say a few words about the above-mentioned Chorus in a reflection of about what it means to **"die to sin" (Rom 6:6 & 11)** below.

CHAPTER TWO

What is Sin?

Sin is a transgression **(missing the mark),** an iniquity, an offence against God and our neighbour.

The type of sins if committed, **(and not confessed),** that do break a relationship with God and neighbour are mentioned below. They will be an obstacle to entry into heaven, especially, if they are not confessed before death. St. Paul says: "Do you not know that wrongdoers will not inherit the Kingdom of God? Do not be deceived:

> **"Fornicators, idolaters, adulterers, male prostitutes, sodomites, thieves, the greedy, drunkards, revilers, robbers – none of these will inherit the Kingdom of God" (1 Cor 6:9-10).**

> **"But as for the cowardly, the faithless, the polluted, the murderers, the fornicators, the sorcerers, the idolaters, and all liars, their place will be in the lake that burns with fire and sulphur, which is the second death" (Rev 21:8).**

In Catholic doctrine, there are other sins which might not be sins considered mortal **(big offences)** but venial sins **(small offences 1 Jn 5:16).** This category of sins falls into the sins of thought, word, deed and omission. The sin of omission can be a mortal sin also. It is advisable to confess them so that they may not lead to bigger offences. In the life in the Spirit we are expected to be in a state of grace always.

Reflection

The **"great change"**, mentioned in the aforementioned above chorus means to **die to sin:**

> **"For if we have been united together in His likeness of death, certainly we also shall be in the likeness of His resurrection, knowing this, that our old man was crucified with Him, that the body of sin might be done away with, that we no longer be slaves of sin. For the death that He died, He died to sin once for all; but the life that He lives, He lives to God" (Rom 6:6).**

The above text from the Letter to the Romans means that Christians are no longer slaves to sin but alive unto God. They are not being controlled by sin any longer but by the Spirit of God. A Scriptural passage explains it better: "So I say, live by the Spirit and you will not gratify the desires of the sinful nature" **(Gal 5:16 NIV).** Christians can still commit sin of course, but are given tremendous power over sin through the **"Life in the Spirit"**. Two Scriptural passages testify to the Christians' power over sin:

> **"There is therefore now no condemnation to those who are in Christ Jesus, who do not walk according to the flesh, but according to the Spirit" (Rom 8:1).**

Jesus stood and cried out, saying "If anyone thirsts, let him come to Me and drink, as the Scripture has said, out of his belly will flow rivers of living water" (Jn 7:37-38).

Water is one of the symbols of the Holy Spirit that is given to Christians to enable them to fight against sin. There is also the sacrament of Reconciliation in the battle against sin.

"Die to sin" is a concept that needs to be explained. When one dies to anything, one becomes inactive to that thing. When we die to sin, it means we are no longer active in committing sin. This does not mean that we cannot sin any longer! No, we are still vulnerable and susceptible to fall into sin. This human vulnerability to fall into sin, no matter how much we try, is called **"concupiscence".** Then, however, we are given amazing graces through the sacraments, especially: the Sacrament of Penance, **(Sacrament of Reconciliation),** Holy Eucharist **(Holy Communion)** and the sacrament of the sick, just to enable us to live holy lives. Living holy lives means **"walking in the light"** 1 John 1 makes this point clear by showing us how to maintain steady and holy lives:

"But if we walk in the light, as he is in the light, we have fellowship with one another, and the blood of Jesus, his Son, purifies us from all sin. If we claim to be without sin, we deceive ourselves and the truth is not in us. If we

confess our sins, He is faithful and just and will forgive us our sins. If we claim we have not sinned, we make Him out to be a liar and His word has no place in our lives" (1 Jn 1:7-10).

The explanation of the above Scripture means that if we fall into serious sins, for any reason at all, we break relationship with God the Father. If we go to Confession to confess them, the relationship with God through Jesus Christ is restored - back on track again i.e., to new life. All sources of "new life" **(living holy lives)** come from Jesus Christ.

From the foregoing explanation of what it means to die to sin, one can now be in a position to determine whether:

One is born again or a new creation, if he or she lives in the Spirit and walks in the Spirit (Gal 5:16), and having Jesus as one's personal Lord and Saviour (Gal 5:16).

The above is the essence of the **"life in the Spirit".**

St. Paul explains the difference between the "Baptism of Repentance" and the "life in the Spirit" as follows:

"And finding some disciples, he said to them, "Did you receive the Holy Spirit when you believed?" So they said to him, "We have not so much as heard whether there is a Holy

Spirit". And he said to them, "Into what then were you baptized?" So they said, "Into John's baptism". Then Paul said, "John indeed baptized with a baptism of repentance, saying to the people, that they should believe in Him who would come after him, that is, on Christ".

When they heard this, they were baptized in the name of the Lord Jesus. This is sacramental baptism as instituted by Jesus Christ. Paul baptized them after he had preached Christ to them. They confessed to Paul that they had John's baptism. Paul wouldn't have repeated John's baptism on the disciples. After this, Paul gave them baptism in the Spirit through the baptism in the name of Jesus and the laying of hands. Paul indeed intended to give them baptism in the Spirit. Let us see the order in which it happened in the Acts of Apostles 19:

Paul asked them to believe in Jesus who was the one to come. They did believe and they were baptized in the name of the Lord Jesus **(Acts 19:5).** This is sacramental baptism. Sacramental baptism precedes baptism in the Spirit for sacramental baptism is the foundation of it. When Paul had laid his hands on them, the Holy Spirit came upon them and they spoke in tongues and prophesied" **(Acts 19:6).** This is baptism in the Spirit. Speaking in tongues and prophesying are features of the baptism in the Spirit which was manifested after the laying on of hands. Baptism in the Spirit precedes sacramental baptism, just like sacramental baptism precedes baptism in the Spirit: so also, confirmation follows after baptism in the churches. Baptism in the Spirit and the Sacrament of Confirmation are conferred by the laying on of hands and they are interconnected. This incident took place in Ephesus.

Another example happened in Samaria in Acts 8:

> **"Now when the apostles at Jerusalem heard that Samaria had accepted the word of God, they sent Peter and John to them. The two went down and prayed for them that they might receive the Holy Spirit (for as yet the Spirit had not come upon any of them; they had only been baptized in the name of the Lord Jesus). Then Peter and John laid their hands on them, and they received the Holy Spirit (Acts 8:14-17).**

Baptism in the Holy Spirit was administered by St. Paul by the laying on of hands and the invocation of the Holy Spirit. While laying hands upon them, he called upon the Holy Spirit to fill them. It is like the Sacrament of Confirmation which needs no pouring of water but conferment from a bishop or a priest appointed by a bishop. It is a fulfilment of the text in **Lk 3:16**,

> **"He will baptize you with the Holy Spirit and fire".**

The reasons why John's baptism does not give entrance into the Kingdom of God

John's baptism does not give entrance into the Kingdom of God and make us new creations. The reason is that Jesus is the door or entrance to heaven; there is no other way! Jesus says: **"I am the Way, and the Truth, (Jn 14:6)** and the Life. No one comes to the Father except through Me". This is the reason why those righteous men and women who died before Jesus had to wait until Jesus had been glorified through the Paschal Mystery **(His Passion, Death, Resurrection, and Ascension into heaven).**

A text from Matthew's Gospel can shed light on this point:

> **"Then Jesus cried again with a loud voice and breathed His last. At that moment the curtain of the temple was torn in two, from top to bottom. The earth shook, and rocks were split. Tombs also were opened, and many bodies of the saints who had fallen asleep were raised. After His resurrection they came out of the tombs and entered the holy city (Jerusalem) and appeared to many. Now when the centurion and those with Him, who were keeping watch over Jesus, saw the earthquake and what took place, they were terrified and said, 'Truly this man was God's Son!'(Mt 27:50-54).**

Reflection

The above text has now made it clear that only Jesus through His **Paschal Mystery** could open the door of heaven. This is the reason why the baptism He commanded is the only one that can make us children of God, members of God's family, and give us entrance to heaven. Another spectacular event that made the centurion and others watching over Jesus confess Jesus as **'Truly this man was God's Son'** was the earthquake that shook the earth, split and terrified the centurion and others.

It is important to write out the text of Christian Baptism as commanded by Jesus here:

> **"Go therefore and make disciples of all nations, baptizing them in the name of the Father and of the Son and of the Holy Spirit, and teaching them to obey everything that I have commanded you. And remember, I am with you always, to the end of the age" (Mt 28:19-20).**

What happens in practice is that after the eight weeks of Life in the Spirit seminars, the participants are commissioned to go out for Jesus on evangelization. During the laying on of hands, the Holy Spirit bathes participants with the Holy Spirit and fire. Some participants' spiritual gifts are manifested at this stage. Others' own gifts manifest during their weekly prayer meetings, especially, at the praise and worship section.

Indeed, the disciples received John's non-sacramental baptism which they confessed that they had received only just that. Paul's intention was to give them baptism in the Spirit. Here I am making reference to Acts 19. This is sacramental baptism instituted by Jesus. After this, Paul laid his hands on them, and the Holy Spirit came upon them and they spoke in tongues and prophesied (Acts 19:6). This is baptism in the Spirit preceding the spiritual gifts of tongues and prophecy. This is the case always with the baptism of the Spirit. Sacramental baptism always precedes baptism in the Spirit. This is because it prepares Christians for the baptism in the Spirit.

Before the case of St. Paul in Ephesus, similar case had happened in Samaria in Acts 8.

> **"Now when the apostles in Jerusalem had accepted the word of God, they sent them Peter and John, who went down and prayed for them, that they might receive the Holy Spirit, for it had not yet fallen upon any of them; they had only been baptized in the name of the Lord Jesus. Then they laid hands on them and they received the Holy Spirit" (Acts 8:14-17).**

This is another example of sacramental baptism that precedes baptism in the Spirit.

God makes use of the hands of His holy men **(especially priests)** in a mysterious way. Simon marvelled at the phenomenon of the laying on of hands that he offered the apostles money in exchange for the gift of laying on hands, but they refused. "But Peter said to him, "May your money perish with you, because you thought that you could buy the gift of God with money ..." (Acts 8:18-21).

At the Eucharistic celebration, a different method of laying on of hands, and calling upon the Holy Spirit at the consecration is used. When the Holy Spirit comes upon the bread and the wine, they are miraculously turned into the Body and the Blood of Christ.

The disciples **(12 in number), (Acts 19: 7),** said, "No, we have not even heard there is a Holy Spirit" **(Acts 19:2).** Paul was talking about the **"baptism in the Spirit"**. Many believers today are still in the same situation as the disciples **(have not heard about the baptism of the Holy Spirit).** This means that many believers are ignorant of **the baptism of the Holy Spirit.** The two examples given above: one at Ephesus, and the other at Samaria, show that the Holy Spirit was given after the sacramental baptism. To them, Pentecostal experiences were peculiar to the early Christians alone. It is not so! God would not be God – God of justice, mercy and faithfulness **(Mt 23:23),** if He distributed His Holy Spirit to the early Christians alone and excluded the later generations. It would mean that the later generations would not serve God effectively. The Holy Spirit's empowerments are referred to as the **"promise of the Father"** in the Acts of Apostles. The early Christians could not do without them; neither can modern Christians. It is the conviction of the Charismatic Renewal that the gifts of the Holy Spirit are part of the full outpouring of the Holy Spirit and what was common in the early church is vital for today's Christians.

A text from the Acts of Apostles can make matters clear here:

> **"While staying with them, He ordered them not to leave Jerusalem, but wait there for the promise of the Father. 'This', He said, 'is what you have heard from me; for John baptized with water but you will be baptized with the Holy Spirit not many days from now"(Acts 1:4-5).**

Divine Revelation
Discernment (revelation) is one of the spiritual gifts. The Church was founded on Peter's confession of Jesus being the Christ, the Son of God:

> **"Simon Peter answered, 'You are the Messiah, the Son of the living God'. And Jesus answered him, 'Blessed are you, Simon son of Jonah! For flesh and blood has not revealed this to you, but my Father in heaven. And I tell you, you are Peter, and on this rock I will build my church and the gates of Hades will not prevail against it" (Mt 16:16-18).**

Spiritual gifts are an important aspect of the Church, as one can see from the Catechism of the Catholic Church:

> **"So that she can fulfil her mission, the Holy Spirit 'bestows upon [the Church] varied hierarchic and charismatic gifts, and in this way directs her" (Catechism of the Catholic Church CCC 768).**

A text from the Bible can help us understand the meaning of revelation or discernment:

> **"The secret things belong to the Lord our God, but the revealed things belong to us and our children for ever, to observe all the words of this law" (Deut 29:29).**

We can now see that spiritual gifts are a great enablement to the Church. They enable the Church to effectively carry out God's instructions on life, especially God's hidden things, **(God's purposes),** which flesh and blood can cannot discern or reveal.

I have been emphatic in my description of the spiritual gifts **(Tongues, prophecies etc).** This is because, I have looked at them from my own point of view, and others whose spiritual lives have been dramatically enhanced spiritually after their baptism of the Holy Spirit **(the Holy Spirit and fire type of life).**

My Personal Experience

I had my **Baptism and Confirmation** in 1957. I remained timid and lukewarm in my Christian life till 1982, when I had the phenomenal experience of **baptism in the Holy Spirit (Holy Spirit and fire).** I received spiritual gifts which enabled me to be dramatically more effective in my Church ministry, evangelisation, love for the Sacred Scriptures, the Eucharist, a deeper love for Jesus and Mary, and ecumenical relations **(my relations with non-Catholics).**

The period of lukewarmness is a slippery slope

This is a period when one's Christian life is neither hot nor cold. Let us have a look at Jesus' own words in the book of Revelation:

> **"I know your works; you are neither cold nor hot. I wish that you were either cold or hot. So, because you are lukewarm and, neither cold nor hot, I am about to spit you out of my mouth"(Rev 3:15-16).**

Reflection

Lukewarmness or indifference in Christianity is the worst thing in the world! If Christianity is worth anything, it is worth everything. An indifferent attitude to Christian living is inexcusable. Jesus does not want believers to be indifferent. Christianity demands the total attention of a believer without reserve. Jesus gives His life without reserve – laying down His life for us. One cannot drink the cup of the Lord and the cup of demons **(1 Cor 10:21).**

> **"No one can serve two masters; for a slave will either hate one and love the other or be devoted to the one and despise the other. You cannot serve God and wealth" (Mt 6:24).**

Christianity is about making a decision for a total surrender of one's life to God, to love Him, serve Him, worship Him in this world and then to enjoy eternity with Him.

A Mystery Remains

It is indeed a mystery the reasons why sanctifying grace did not become manifest in active Church activities till my baptism in the Holy Spirit in 1982 - a period of 25 years (1957-1982). On this point, I thought wrongly, that it was the Holy Spirit who was dormant in me! I discussed it with our parish priest, Rev. Fr. Con Boyle, and he said it was the human spirit that was dormant and not the Holy Spirit. The **boldness and empowerments** I received from the life in the Holy Spirit is overwhelming!

The above phenomenal experience is not peculiar to me alone, but is for all who went through the eight weeks of **"Life in the Spirit"** seminars in the Charismatic Movement. The Apostles and the disciples remained fearful until the **"the promise of the Father",** the manifestation of the Holy Spirit's empowerments, came in the form of the Holy Spirit and fire. My greatest desire is to encourage other Christians to seek life in the Holy Spirit. The promise of the Holy Spirit is also meant for the new generations also **(Joel 2:28),** even today!

CHAPTER THREE

The fresh outpouring of Pentecost is a continuous event

There are two extracts from the history of the Catholic Charismatic Renewal below which show that it is indeed a continuous event:

The renewal of this experience of "Baptism in the Spirit" began in the Catholic Church in February 1967, when a group of students on retreat at Duquesne University began praying for a fresh outpouring of Pentecost. Many of them had profound "Baptism in the Spirit" experiences and they shared these experiences with others in prayer.

This Renewal of "Baptism in the Spirit" has "set on fire" for the Lord nine million Catholic charismatics in the U.S. and 150 million Catholic charismatics worldwide. These are only a part of the 600 million witnesses, through Baptism in the Holy Spirit, throughout all denominations worldwide!

What an outpouring of the Spirit in a little over 40 years! Many Catholics having experienced this "Baptism in the Spirit" – this renewal of the sacraments of Baptism and Confirmation – have become more involved in their parishes, community outreaches, teen ministry and missionary work" (History of the Roman Catholic Charismatic Renewal, Immaculata Center, Diocese of Lafayette, LA 7051): (searched on 14 May 2015).

One of the important things that comes out from the second extract above is that the writer is saying that **"baptism in the Spirit"** is a renewal of Baptism and Confirmation. The Spirit is always active. It is human nature that is normally dormant or sleeping after Baptism and Confirmation. It is good to clear up one fact here. It is the same Holy Spirit we received in Baptism and Confirmation that we also can receive in the **"baptism in the Spirit"**. One of the reasons for human nature being normally dormant or sleeping after **Baptism and Confirmation** is the non-practising of Christian duties. I have said above that it is a mystery the human spirit being dormant after **Baptism and Confirmation**. **Baptism** is always the gift of the Holy Spirit and is the foundational and abiding sacrament of Christian life.

St. Paul talked about fanning into flame our gifts of the Holy Spirit, in both his first and second letters to Timothy:

> **"Do not neglect the gift you have which was given you by prophetic utterance when the elders laid their hands upon you. Practise these duties, devote yourself to them, so that all may see your progress. Take heed to yourself and to your teaching; hold to that, for by so doing you will save both yourself and your hearers". "This is why I am reminding you now to fan into a flame the gift that God gave you when I laid hands on you. God's gift was not a spirit of timidity,**

but the Spirit of power, and love, and self-control" (1 Tim 4: 14 ; 2 Tim 1:6-7).

As one can gather from the above quotation, the Holy Spirit is not a spirit of fear, but of power. Why is this power of the Holy Spirit silent or dormant, after receiving the Holy Spirit in Baptism and Confirmation? Confirmation indeed is intended to specifically manifest the **power and fire** of the Holy Spirit. The reason why human nature is dormant or sleeping after Baptism and Confirmation is difficult to pinpoint. One cannot definitively give accurate reasons from the things of God unless revealed **(Deut 29:29).** Two reasons are considered here: (1) It needs to be fanned into flame by virtuous Christian practices; (2) It needs to be prayed for! Desirously asked for! The second of these was what the students of Duquesne University did in 1967 – praying for the release of the Spirit.

The release of the Spirit, the fresh outpouring of Pentecost, needs to be prayed for. As I said above, that was what the students on retreat at Duquesne University did: i.e. praying for it. This is one of the reasons why 8 weeks life in the Spirit seminars and trainings are normally undertaken by Catholic Charismatics as often as possible. We did one in the 19 Catholic Charismatic Renewals in London. Many spiritual gifts, mentioned in **1 Cor 12:8-10** were manifested among participants, including the gifts of tongues, prophecy, healings, interpretation, and interpretation of tongues etc.

The purpose for the giving of the Holy Spirit
Who is the Holy Spirit?

The Holy Spirit is a Person. He is the Third Person of the Blessed Trinity. Just like we have a personal relationship with God the Father through the Son, we also have a personal relationship with the Holy Spirit through the Son who is the Mediator **between God and us (1 Tim 2:5).**

The Holy Spirit is frequently referred to as "The **Paraclete" (The Helper or Personal Friend); "Advocate"** (One who stands for us in cases of problems). He is our **Most Intimate** Friend, as we can see from the two Biblical references below:

> **"I will not leave you orphans; I will come to you. But the Helper, the Holy Spirit, whom the Father will send in my My name, He will teach you all things, and bring to your remembrance all that I said to you" (Jn 14:18; Jn 14:26).**

> **"And I will pray the Father, and He will give you another Helper, that He may abide with you for ever – the Spirit of truth, whom the world cannot receive, because it neither sees Him, nor knows Him; but you know Him, for He dwells with you and will be in you" (Jn 14:16-17).**

The second reference above makes mention of **another "Helper"** or **"Advocate":** Jesus is the first Helper and the second Helper is the Holy Spirit. The Holy Spirit helps us to know Jesus as our personal Lord and Saviour. He also helps us to remember His doctrine of salvation **(1 Cor 12:3; Jn 14:26).**

One of God's purposes in the outpouring of the Holy Spirit is to empower believers to go out **boldly** and spread the Gospel, and to witness with their own lives. The needs for which God gave the Holy Spirit to the Church in the early days are still the same today. Jesus told His disciples, "But you will receive power when the Holy Spirit has come upon you, and you will be my witnesses in Jerusalem, in all Judea and Samaria, and to the ends of the earth" **(Acts 1: 8).**

There is a note on **Acts 1:8** in the New King James Study Bible which makes it very clear the purpose of the outpouring of the Holy Spirit. I would like to quote it verbatim (word for word) here:

> **"Acts 1:8 Christ's Final Charter and promise, WORLD EVANGELISM: In five NT references, Jesus directly charges His disciples to go and preach the Gospel to all the world (Matt 28:18-20; Mark 16:15-18; Luke 24:45-48; John 20:21-23; Acts 1:8). Here His Great Commission is preceded by His promise of the outpouring of the Holy Spirit. Empowerment of world evangelism is tied inseparably to this promise. There is obvious need for power if people are to fully perceive the Gospel, but prior to that, another issue**

awaits resolution. The Spirit has come to convince us to go. We need power to serve effectively, to heal the sick, and deliver those possessed of unclean spirits. But let us receive the Holy Spirit's first anointing-power to act - to go. Then, He will give us

(1) power to find the lost;

(2) authority to boldly declare Jesus as the Son of God; and

(3) power to establish His church — locally and worldwide.

The intended borders of expansion are clear: Jerusalem (local), Judea (national), Samaria (cross-cultural) and "end of the earth" (international). Jesus' last earthly command points to His power and His pathways for global evangelism"

(John 20:21-23/Acts 4:12) G .C (Spirit-Filled Life Bible New KJV 1991, p.1623).

One particular reason why we are timid to practise our faith **boldly** in our workplaces, streets, every nook and corner of our country, is that the Holy Spirit is yet to be released in us. The apostles and disciples were timid in the Upper Room, but on the Pentecost day when fresh outpouring of the Holy Spirit and fire came upon them, their timidity vanished like smoke! They were **exceptionally bold!** Peter's wonderful **homily** penetrated into the hearts of the congregation and three thousand converts were made that day! In order for people to become Christian they had to be **'baptised'** and in the conventional sense of Christian baptism **(Acts 2:41).**

All of them received the gifts of tongues and prophecy. The impediment through fear to going out boldly and spreading the Good News was removed! They went everywhere proclaiming the gospel of Jesus Christ.

Gifts of the Holy Spirit
The Sevenfold Gifts of the Holy Spirit are bestowed anew with the Sacrament of Confirmation.

The Sevenfold Gifts of the Holy Spirit are:
(1) Wisdom; (2) Understanding; (3) Counsel; (4) Fortitude; (5) Knowledge; (6) Piety (some theologians refer to this as "Spirit of Godliness); and (7) the Spirit of the Fear of the Lord ("Is 11:2-3: Catechism of the Catholic Church CCC 1831")

The last one, the "**Fear of the Lord**" needs to be explained. It does not mean that we should be terrified at the mentioning of God. It means the awesomeness, majesty, adoration, worship that belongs to God alone. It means **Reverence** that is due to Him alone, God almighty, the God of hosts. Sometimes, Scripture can be used to explain Scripture, for example, Job says, "And He said to man, "Behold, "**The fear of the Lord, that is wisdom, and to shun evil is understanding" (Job 28:28). This is Job's definition of the fear of the Lord from the Bible.** Fearing God also means avoiding evil and wickedness. "Fear God and keep His commandments for this is the whole duty of man" **(Ecc 12:13).** God Himself commends Job by saying ... "There is no one on earth like Job; he is blameless and upright, **a man who fears God and shuns evil" (Job 1:8).**

The Spiritual Gifts (1 Cor 12:7-10) according to St. Paul
There are 9 Spiritual or Charismatic gifts which are usually manifested during the Life in the Spirit seminars.
They are:

      1. Wisdom; 2. Word of knowledge; 3. Faith;

      4. Healing; 5. Working of miracles;

      6. Prophecy; 7. Discernment of spirits;

      8. Different kinds of Tongues; and

      9. Interpretation of Tongues.

Reflection on the spiritual gifts
For sake of the economy of time and space, only two of the gifts will be here reflected upon: (1) the gift of prophecy, and (2) the gift of tongues.

Gift of Prophecy defined:
Prophecy is the speech **(oracle of God)** through the words of man. It is God's divine plan concerning future events for God's people. God does not do anything without first of all revealing it to His prophets, for example, "Surely the Sovereign Lord does nothing without revealing His plan to His servants the prophets" **(Amos 3:7).**

God indeed knows the end from the beginning **(Is 46:10)**. A good example comes from Isaiah, about the infancy of Jesus:

> **"There is a child born for us, a son given to us and dominion laid on His shoulders; and this is the name they gave Him: Wonder-Counsellor, Mighty-God (EL-GIBHOR). Eternal-Father, Prince-of-Peace" (Is 9:6).**

The verb to **"prophesy"** is to say what God says as in **Ezekiel 37:**

> **"Then He said to me, "Prophesy to these bones and say to them, 'Dry bones, hear the word of the LORD! This is what the Sovereign LORD says to these bones: I will make breath enter you and you will come to life" (Ezekiel 37:4-5).**

Ezekiel's prophecy is a perfect example of a prophet not speaking his own words but God's. This is also supported by a text from the Second Letter of St. Peter, as can be seen below:

> **"And so we have the prophetic word confirmed, which you do well to heed as a light that shines in a dark place, until the day dawns and the morning star rises in your hearts; knowing this first, that no prophecy of Scripture is of any private interpretation, for prophecy never came by the will of man,**

but holy men of God spoke as they were moved by the Holy Spirit" (2 Pt 1:19-20).

From the above Scripture, it is clearly seen that prophecy is entirely the action of the Holy Spirit, through holy men of God. In the Old Testament, similar Holy Spirit activities happened! Some theologians call these activities an Old Testament **"Pentecost" (outpouring of the Holy Spirit).** God took some of the Spirit that was on Moses and placed it upon seventy elders, and they prophesied! **(Nums 11:25).**

An extract from 1 Samuel will shed light on the fact that no prophet speaks his own words:

"Then the Spirit of the Lord will possess you and you will be in a prophetic frenzy along with them and be turned into a different person" i.e. it will not be himself but the Spirit in him prophesying" (1 Sam 10:6).

As I said above, the Spirit employs the faculty of a prophet and speaks the prophet's language through him. This is one of God's marvels that happened on the Pentecost day – the phenomenon of new language.

The benefits of the Gift of Prophecy

This gift enables the people of God to live an authentic, frank, truthful and reliable way of life. This is because prophecy, or oracle of God, is God's word through His prophet, acting as light for His people. It tells people about future events, warning them about dangers ahead and how to live righteous lives in obedience to God's instruction. Simply put, this means to follow up God's marked ways of life, fulfilling God's commands to love God and neighbour.

CHAPTER FOUR

Gift of Tongues Glossolalia (Greek)

Gift of Tongues defined: "Glosso" means "word" and "lalia" means speaking. Jesus refers to this gift as **"a sign"** and **"new tongues"**. Rev. Fr. Michael Scanlon of St. Mary's, West Croydon calls it **"a new language"**. He said this when he was giving a talk at the **"Life in the Spirit Seminar". It is a new language!**

This gift of new language occurs as a result of the outpouring or indwelling of the Holy Spirit. This phenomenon is described in a section of the King James Bible Study and it is quoted here below:

> By "a process of yielding the complete person" the Pentecostal or Charismatic does not mean either (a) a passivity of mind or (2) a self-hypnotic or trance-like state. Rather, this terminology refers to an assertive prayerful, heartfelt quest for God. "The mind is active, worshipping Jesus Christ, the Baptizer with the Holy Spirit (Jn 1:33). The emotions are warmed, as the love of God is poured forth into our hearts (Rom 5:5).
>
> One's physical being participates, worship is spoken and expressed, with upraised voice in prayer (Acts 4:24) or upraised hands of adoration"

(Ps. 63:1-5) by Paul Walker Holy Spirit Gifts and Power, Spirit-Filled Life Bible, New King James Version, 1991, p.202.

Reflection

I would like to clarify an extract or a phrase from the above reference:

"an assertive prayerful, heartfelt quest for God". This quest for God **(the desire deep within the heart of a believer)** makes the **"baptism of the Holy Spirit (outpouring of the Holy Spirit and a new life in the Spirit)** happen. Jesus sees this great desire and baptizes the believer with the Holy Spirit **(Jn 1:33).**

My personal experience (witness)

Another way to look at the phenomenon of the **"outpouring or indwelling of the Holy Spirit"** is that, a believer becomes so filled **(outpouring)** with the Holy Spirit. Then the whole faculty of the believer is controlled **(employed by the Spirit),** and then, the Spirit speaks through the believer. This is a situation where a believer bursts into speaking an irresistible language, as given to him or her by the Holy Spirit. Below is the story of how I received the **"baptism of the Holy Spirit"**:

I went to Lagos, in Southwest Nigeria from the North and happened to be at the Church of Assumption, Falomo, Lagos. Praises and worship activities were going on at a Catholic Charismatic Group. Many people were speaking in tongues. It was after I had been in the Catholic Charismatic Movement for only a few months. It was a new experience to me. I became filled with the desire to speak in tongues but, nothing happened! I did not speak in tongues! I went back to the North and I had three days of fasting and praying, asking God to give me the gift of tongues.

I went back to Lagos on the 2nd of January, 1982. I was alone in a small room at Obalende in the early morning of the 3rd of January 1982. I was questioning God in my heart, saying, Lord "why am I not given this gift of tongues"? While I was still wondering why, the Spirit started spinning me round and round the small room. I stayed alone and I started speaking in tongues! I had a gift of prophecy, a gift of tongues and a gift of the word of knowledge at the same time **1 Cor 12:8-11).** This is how my **"baptism in the Holy Spirit"** came. Different people had different experiences. It is real and wonderful!

Reflection
God our Father is highly approachable. If you have done all you think that is necessary according to the Sacred Scriptures - **(the requirements for asking (Mt 7:7, etc)),** - then, personally approach Him with your queries! He says, "Put Me in remembrance: Let us contend together; State your case, that you may be acquitted" **(Is 43:26).** Jacob insisted on God blessing him and God did. He blessed him and gave him a new name **"Israel"** and made him great beyond measure! **"Israel"** is a new name for Christians, the new people of God. A new name is promotional and a symbol of divine prosperity. So Jacob called the name of the place Peniel: "For I have seen God face, to face and my life is preserved" **(Gen 32:30).** This shows God our Father's preparedness to give us everything we confidently ask Him in faith. Two passages from Sacred Scripture support this:

> "For the Lord God is a sun and shield; The Lord will give grace and glory; No good thing will He withhold from those who walk uprightly" (Ps 84:11).
>
> "He who did not spare His own Son, but delivered Him up for us all, how shall He not with Him also freely give us all things" (Rom 8:32).

From the above two references from the Bible, I can confidently say that God our Father can benevolently grant us all things.

Gift of Tongues is for every baptized Christian!

Many Catholic Christians have already made up their minds that the gift of Tongues is not for every Christian. Of course, lack of faith could be an obstacle to receiving the gift. It is also for the present generation according to **Joel 2:28-29.** This generation referred to by Joel could also mean the generation in Apostolic times and generation yet to come. The Pentecost accounts in Acts 2 have enough proofs that show the gift of Tongues is for all baptized Christians. There are different theological opinions on the matter but I believe that there is scriptural support to believe that all Christians can participate in the gift of tongues. People differ greatly in faith matters. Without faith no one can please God **(Heb 11:6).**

Jesus says

"I will do whatever you ask in my name, so that the Father may be glorified in the Son. If in my name you ask me for anything, I will do it" (Jn 14:13-14).

These proofs are evident in **Acts 2:1, and 4:**

"When the Day of Pentecost had fully come, they were all with one accord in one place. And they were all filled with the Holy Spirit and began to speak with other tongues, as the Holy Spirit gave them utterance" (Acts 2:1, 4).

When Paul had laid hands on them, the Holy Spirit came upon them, and they spoke with tongues and prophesied (Acts 19: 2-6). This was when St. Paul administered the baptism of the Holy Spirit on the 12 disciples (Acts 19:2-6) and all of them prophesied and spoke in tongues" (Acts 19:2-6).

The above quotation needs to be explained. Here Paul administered sacramental baptism which precedes baptism in the Spirit. "When they heard this, they were baptized in the name of the Lord Jesus" (Acts 19:5), a case of sacramental baptism. "And when Paul laid his hands on them, the Holy Spirit came upon them, and they spoke in tongues and prophesied" (Acts 19:6), a clear case of the baptism in the Spirit.

Reflection

The note on **Acts 2:1 "with one accord"** means homothumadon (Greek), "Being unanimous, having mutual consent, being in agreement, having group unity, having one mind and purpose".

Now, from the above reasons – one accord, group unity, one mind, one purpose as given above, support the claim that the gift is meant for all. **"Meant for all";** in the sense that Jesus addresses it as one of the signs that will accompany those who believe **(Mk 16:17).** It is possible for anyone who believes in Jesus Christ to have the gift. Jesus dies for all but it is those who believe in Him that will have His salvation. Jesus, being the Baptizer and Giver of the Holy Spirit and the Holy Spirit's gifts, it would be unthinkable to deprive any of the believers gathered in the Upper Room of the Gift of Tongues!

In verse 4, it reads, "And they were all filled with the Holy Spirit and began to speak with other tongues, as the Spirit gave them utterance".

The three things that happened here confirm that the gift of tongues is for every baptised Christian:

 (1) All were filled with the Holy Spirit,
(2) All began to speak with other tongues,
(3) All received the Holy Spirit's utterance.

Before, I continue with other features of the Gift of Tongues, I would like to quote, in addition to Biblical evidence evidenced above, from Rev. Fr. B.M Heron's book on Catholic Charismatic Renewal to support my claim:

> **"This claim is made by bishops and learned theologians as also by people who cannot read and children under ten. In the face of so much evidence it is surely difficult to deny that very many Christians, including largely Catholics, have been spiritually helped by receiving the gift of tongues. Some years ago it was estimated that at least 700,000 Catholics in the USA prayed in tongues, so it will be seen that this is not a rare gift for just a few people"**
> (Heron, B.M, 1992:13)

The claim Rev. Fr. Benedict M. Heron is making is that the **"Gift of Tongues"** is not a rare gift for just a few people. I quoted it to support my claim that the Gift of Tongues is within the reach of every baptized Christian. Lack of faith and ignorance (lack of knowledge of the spiritual value of the gift of Tongues) could be an obstacle to receiving the gift of Tongues. God willingly offered His only Begotten Son for our salvation but no one can have that salvation without faith, even though, it is meant for everybody. In the Gospel of Mark where Jesus says, **"these signs"** will follow those who believe; it is only the gift of tongues **(new language),** that He mentioned out of the nine spiritual gifts.

The Gift of Tongues is an Identity of every Christian

From the lips of Jesus Himself we can agree with the proof from the Gospel of St. Mark:

> **"And these signs will follow those who believe: In My name they will cast out demons; they will speak with new tongues; they will take up serpents; and if they drink anything deadly, it will by no means hurt them; they will lay hands on the sick, and they will recover" (Mk 16:17-18).**

However, this is not to say that unless one has the gift of tongues, he or she is not a good Christian. Far from that, there are so many gifts of the Holy Spirit, and it is possible for one to have one without the others. In other words one can have another gift, without having the gift of tongues. Nevertheless I encourage believers to pray and earnestly desire for the gift of tongues and God will grant their earnest yearnings for the gift of Tongues. I am expressing my individual experience of view of the gift of tongues. People differ in faith matters and spirituality. This is one reason why God in His divine providence gives us a variety of gifts.

Reflection of the above reference

Jesus' opening sentence **"And these signs** will follow those who believe" automatically, makes it an identity for every believer (a Christian). Anyone who believes in Christ Jesus can have these signs. Believers as a body will manifest these gifts (at least in apostolic times and always). The other statement **"if they drink anything deadly..."** should be carefully considered that we should not be presumptuous about carelessly taking drinks anyhow. What Jesus means here is that, if any wicked person wants to intentionally kill a Christian, he or she would fail. One would ask, **"what of the martyrs, are they not Christians"?**

The case of the martyrs is quite different. The death of the martyrs glorifies God. Martyrdom is a special privilege granted to the martyrs whose deaths are really like that of Jesus! Like Jesus willingly accepted death on the cross **(Phil 2:8),** so also, did the martyrs. They are in a special place with Jesus, as we can see from a text quoted from Revelation:

> **"I answer him, 'You can tell me, my lord', Then he said, 'These are the people who have been through the great persecution, and because they have washed their robes white again in the blood of the Lamb, they now stand in front of God's throne and serve him day and night in His sanctuary; and the One who sits on the throne will spread his tent over them" (Rev 7:14-15).**

To support my claim that **"no wicked person can intentionally kill a Christian" unless Jesus allows it** mentioned above; I would like to quote below the conversation of St. Bridget with Jesus during a riot in Rome:

> **During a riot at Rome, a mob came to the house where St. Bridget lived: a leader talked of burning Bridget alive. She prayed to Our Lord to know if she should flee to safety. Jesus advised her to stay: "It doesn't matter if they plot Your death. My power will break the malice of Your enemies: if Mine crucified Me, it is because I permitted it"**
> **(Pieta Book page 16 Divine Mercy Publications Maryville, Skerries, Co. Dublin, Ireland)**

Another example I would like to give here, is an attempt to kill St. Benedict that failed:

On a pedestal to the right of St. Benedict is the poisoned cup, shattered when he made the sign of the cross over it. On a pedestal to the left is a raven about to carry away a loaf of poisoned bread that a jealous enemy had sent to St. Benedict "Saints Who Battled Satan" Paul Thigpen, (2006:51).

Having "made a case" Biblically and by testimonial evidence, that the gift of Tongues is for every baptized Christian, how is it, yet, that every baptized Christian is not receiving the gift?

Difficulties in receiving the gift of Tongues and solutions
Wrong decision:
This may sound emphatic! I have already said that I am looking at things from my individual point of view prompted by personal experience. One of the difficulties is that some believers have made a decision within their hearts, and concluded, and stamped it that **"the gift of Tongues is for early Christians only"**. For this category of believers, the desire to receive "the Gift of Tongues" becomes dead in their hearts. It is the desire in the heart of a believer that God honours and fulfils **(Ps 145:19).**

The heart is the centre of a person's life, the seat of affections, will, desire, emotions, mind, reason, and understanding. Unless we open our hearts to anything we want to receive from God, we will not receive it.
"For with the heart one believes unto righteousness..." (Rom 10:10).

Three things we learn from Sacred Scripture above, 1. Our hearts can make us believe a wrong or right thing; 2. People differ in faith matters; 3. Our hearts **must** be open in order to receive God's divine blessings. This is my own point of view. There are people out there who would not even like anything at all about the gift of Tongues.

Persistency and diligence: Taking the words of our Lord Jesus Christ into our lives, and acting upon them, will surely lead us to receive anything our Father God destined to give us.

For example, His words according to Matthew's Gospel which I quote:

> **"Then the disciples came to Jesus privately and said, "Why could we not cast it out?". So Jesus said to them, "Because of your unbelief; for assuredly, I say to you, if you have faith as a mustard seed, you will say to this mountain, 'Move from here to there', and it will move; and nothing will be impossible to you" (Mt 17:20).**

Praise God! A statement from the above reference **("nothing shall be impossible to you")** sums up all that needs to be said here. Persistency and diligence is the key in prayer that procures God's positive answers, refusing to give up, no matter what happens. Of course, your persistency and diligence must be with ardent faith. "For without faith it is impossible to please God" **(Heb 11:6).** Jacob in Gen 32, **"I will not go unless you bless me"** ..., is an example of persistency. He gave a testimony that he had seen God face to face" **(Gen 32:26-30).** What can we say about these things now? **"The Gift of Tongues"** is for every Christian except for those who do not want it in the first place! This is my personal opinion. There are different theological opinions on the matter but I believe there is scriptural support to believe that all Christians can participate in the gift of tongue. There is nothing we cannot receive from God, if we do not give up! **"And let us not grow weary while doing good, for in due season we shall reap if we do not lose heart" (Gal 6:9).** This means simply that constancy in our prayer is the key to anything we want from God. Jesus' parable in Lk 18:1-8, is about constancy in prayer.

Another example of constancy of prayer is St. Monica's prayer. According to Catholic tradition, she had a difficult unbelieving husband, a worldly son, and a nagging mother-in-law. She continued to pray, fasting and praying, until her son was delivered from his debauchery style of living and later became a bishop, St. Augustine of Hippo **(354 AD).** Both the husband and her mother-in-law all converted as a result of fervent and persistent prayer. There is a **"slogan"** for constancy in prayer called **"PUSH"** means pray until something happens.

Other features of "the Gift of Tongues"
There are two functions of **"the Gift of Tongues"** (1) personal edification, and (2) public exhortation. **"The Gift of Tongues"** is looked at as a **"sign of the presence of the Holy Spirit"** or **"the outpouring or indwelling of the Holy Spirit".** Jesus prophesied it as a sign, saying **"These signs will follow those who believe" (Mk 16:17).** The Gift of Tongues is the only one Jesus mentions as a **"sign"** out of the nine spiritual gifts. It is the way I personally look at it. It has been said above that the **"The Gift of Tongues"** is a sign of the presence of the Holy Spirit. So, when Jesus says **"These signs will follow those who believe"**, it means that the Holy Spirit's presence will follow those who

believe, confirming their miracles along with them. A Biblical reference from the Letter to Hebrews also supports this:

> **"God Himself confirmed their witness with signs and marvels and miracles of all kinds, and by freely giving the gifts of the Holy Spirit" (Heb 2:4).**

CHAPTER FIVE

Self-Edification (1 Cor 14:4; Eph 6:18 and Jude v.20) and Public Exhortation

Permanent personal Indwelling of the Holy Spirit

Jesus confirms it, **"He who believes in Me,** as the Scripture has said, out of his heart will flow rivers of living water" **(Jn 7:38).** It is from the indwelling of the Holy Spirit that a speaker speaks in Tongues. In some cases a believer who speaks in Tongues can speak it normally like he/she speaks other languages, without being provoked by praises and worship. This is because the **"living water"** is the symbol of the Holy Spirit and Fire, the reason **"for the Gift of Tongues".** The living water that is permanent in a believer enables the believer to speak automatically in Tongues when he/she wants.

Facilitator of the use of other spiritual gifts

"The Gift of Tongues" means praying in the Spirit **(Eph 6:17; 1 Cor 14:15; Col 3:16; Eph 5:18),** and because of this, it facilitates the other eight spiritual gifts **(1 Cor 12:8-10)** to manifest and function properly. St Paul says in **Rom 8:26-27,** that the Spirit makes intercession for us with groaning which cannot be uttered, that it is the Spirit who knows the mind of God. This Spirit who knows the mind of God indwells believers. This Spirit empowers the believer and enables him/her to accomplish whatever God wants a believer to do.

A level of holiness is attained

The permanent indwelling of the Holy Spirit in **"the Gift of Tongues",** as explained above, makes a believer who speaks in Tongues frequently achieve a level of holiness. This is because it is the Holy Spirit who prays in the believer who prays in Tongues. Jesus baptizes Christians with the Holy Spirit and Fire which abide with the believer who speaks in tongues forever. John's Baptism with water does not make an indelible mark in the heart of a believer but Christian Baptism, that is, the Baptism made with the sign of the **cross (in the name of the Father, the Son and the Holy Spirit)** does. Sacramental Baptism gives the mark of the indelible character in the heart of a believer. **Baptism of the "Holy Spirit and Fire"** does not give indelible character. The reason for this is that an indelible character on the soul cannot be repeated. Personal love for God and neighbour is enhanced because the whole foundation of **"the Gift of Tongues"** is built on love **(1 Cor 14:1).**

A perfect spiritual weapon for spiritual battles

This is because he who prays in Tongues prays in the Spirit. On this point Sacred Scripture says:

> **"The Spirit too comes to help us in our weakness, For when we cannot choose words in order to pray properly, the Spirit Himself expresses our plea in a way that can never be put into words, and God   who**

knows everything in our hearts knows perfectly well what He means, and that the pleas of the saints expressed by the Spirit are according to the mind of God"(Rom 8:26-27).

The above reference is self-explanatory. Two more references from Sacred Scripture are quoted below:

"And then you must accept salvation from God to be your helmet and receive the word of God from the Spirit to use as a sword. Pray all the time, asking for what you need, praying in the Spirit on every possible occasion. Never get tired of staying awake to pray for all the saints" (Eph 6:17-18).

Writing out the reference: 1 Cor 14:14-15 separately will remove the problem of "mind being unproductive", as Paul clears up the problem of unproductiveness of the mind below:
For if I pray in a tongue, my spirit prays but my mind is unproductive (1 Cor 14:14).

What should I do then? I will pray with the spirit, but I will pray with the mind also; I will sing praise with the spirit, but I will sing praise with the mind also (1 Cor 14:14 -15)

Reflection

Judging from 1 Cor 14:14 about the mind being unproductive, Paul was expressing the dilemma of human mind being unproductive before the mind of God. Praying in tongues without understanding is, of course, a **"limitation"! This "limitation"** has been made up for with the gift of interpretation of tongues (1 Cor 12:10). The gift of interpretation of tongues cancels out the limitation, for the Holy Spirit does not give gifts with limitations!

Different experiences

This section **(Self-edification)** has a variety of experiences:

Individual experiences

There are very many different vocabularies **(utterances)** in **"the Gift of Tongues"**. Believers' experiences in self-edification are very different; for each person according to how the Holy Spirit sees fit. Though, it is Spirit language, it is being perfected and familiarised daily. Although the experiences are different, they serve the same purpose – **glorification of God.**

Singing in the Spirit (Eph 5:19; Eph 5:18; Col 3:16; 1 Col 14:15)

Singing in the Spirit is a marvel in the spirit realm. No same believers sing the same song. Different kinds of song are being sung, but, again, they serve the same purpose – **glorification of God.** When a group of worshippers sing harmoniously in a deep heated praises-and-worship atmosphere, the Spirit moves mightily in a deep ecstasy: people laughing, screaming, crying profusely, shedding tears and others steadily calm. In such a spiritually charged atmosphere, people were being healed and new spiritual gifts manifested.

Personal witness

In my 32 years experience of living **"the Life in the Spirit"**, particularly, **"the Gift of Tongues",** I have discovered that:

It has enhanced **(promoted)** my other gifts, my love for God and neighbour, my love for Jesus and Mary, the Scriptures & religious studies, the Eucharist, love for the service of God, and the desire to serve God more and more. My gift of prophecy, especially, in terms of discerning the spirits of prophecy; and my gift of the word of knowledge, in terms of discernment, improves. This is because when one prays in the Spirit **(praying in Tongues) (1 Cor 14:15),** it is difficult for unclean spirits to confuse it. This is because the Holy Spirit prays through the one who prays in Tongues. Unclean spirits can easily confuse us and deceive us with the spirits of lies when we pray in our normal languages. It will help to clarify the idea of **"praying in spirit"** by writing out fully the text as quoted above:

> **"For if I pray in a tongue, my spirit prays but my mind is unproductive. What should I do**

72

then? I will pray with the spirit, but I will pray with the mind also; I will sing praise with the spirit, but I will sing praise with the mind also" (1 Cor 14:14-15).

Warning against pride in Self-edification

These qualities of Self-edification are given by the Holy Spirit to prepare the believer for the glorification of God; though at the same time useful to himself or herself, and to the Church. It should not in any way make the believer proud! Humility is always the best virtue in the eyes of God.

Public Exhortation

The Gift of Tongues edifies the church as a whole in public worship. Exhortation means a religious advice in a community life, an earnest appeal for good conduct. According to St. Paul **"the Gift of Tongues" and "the Gift of Prophecy"** are built on love **(1 Cor 14:1).** He singled out these two spiritual gifts of the nine gifts mentioned in **1 Cor 12:8-10** and exhorted people of God about good conduct. Right from the Old Testament, God led His people in a community, gave instructions for life and guided them by a pillar of cloud by day and by night a pillar of fire **(Exodus 13:21).** The purpose of public exhortation is essentially orderliness and decency. In the New Testament it is the same purpose.

At Pentecost God showered His blessings in the form of: Fire, the Holy Spirit, and New Language **("the Gift of Tongues")** and these blessings are the fulfilment of **"the baptism of the Holy Spirit" (Jn 1:33).** "The Gift of Tongues" is referred to: as a **"New Language"** because, all the other spiritual gifts happened in the olden days. The Gift of Tongues occurred at Pentecost, in the New Testament era and so it is a new language. So, the **"Gift of Tongues"** can be safely called, **"the Holy Spirit language",** without contradiction or fear of heresy! This is the one of the reasons why human beings cannot understand it. In the olden days, God spoke to stubborn people in strange languages **(foreign languages)** so that they could not understand **them (Is 28:11-12; Deut 28:49-51),** as can be seen from the next paragraph below:

It was decisive on the Pentecost Day of the Holy Spirit to open the languages of the world to hearing and understanding each other's languages in response to ecstatic prayer in praise of God, interpreted in Acts 2:6 and 11 as speaking in foreign languages, symbolizing the worldwide mission of the Church. The Old Testament version of blockage to understanding was prophesied by Isaiah against those who refused to hear, believe or listen to God as can be seen below:

> **"Yes, with stammering lips and in a strange language he will speak to this people, to whom he said: "This is the resting place, give**

rest to the weary; And this is the place of repose" - but they refuse to hear (Is 28:11-12)

Jesus in His teaching of the Parable of the Sower says:

"This is why I speak to them in parables, because 'they look but do not see and hear but do not listen or understand'. Isaiah's prophecy is fulfilled in them, which says:

> **"You shall indeed hear but not understand, you shall indeed look but never see" (Mt 13:13-14)**

Jesus cited Isaiah 28:11-12 as quoted above.

Paul also makes reference to lack of understanding by saying:
What Israel was seeking it did not attain, but the elect attained it, the rest were hardened, as it is written:

> **"God gave them a spirit of deep sleep, eyes that should not see and ears that should not hear, down to this very day" (Rom 11:8)**

In the main chapter for the Gift of Tongues, 1 Cor 14 Paul says:
> **"By people speaking strange tongues and by the lips of foreigners I will speak to this people and even so they will not listen to me, says the Lord (1 Cor 14:21).**

This last reference precedes Paul's saying that:

"Thus, tongues are a sign not for those who believe but for unbelievers, whereas prophecy is not for unbelievers but for those who believe (1 Cor 14:22).

Paul is not actually saying that the Gift of Tongues is not beneficial to a believer! His concern is orderliness of Christian meetings. **He who speaks in tongues speaks mysteries – praises to God (1 Cor 14:2)** He says: "Thank God that I speak in tongues more than anyone else" **(1 Cor 14:18)** What he means is that it is a sign to change an unbeliever to a believer when an unbeliever accepts the message of the Gospel of Christ. Jews refer to non-Jews as unbelievers **(Gentiles).**

On the Pentecost Day the impediments to understanding strange **(foreign)** languages were broken when the Gift of Tongues **(new language)** was given by the Holy Spirit. When a person receives a gift of tongues that person starts to speak mysteries to God. In Acts 10:44-49: From the baptism of Cornelius: **We see the marvels of the Gift of Tongues being "a sign" to unbeliever** "for they could hear them speaking in tongues and glorifying God" **(Acts 10:46).**

Nevertheless difficulty in understanding the meaning of the Gift of Tongues does not affect its effectiveness and the edification that come from it. The main objective of it is the glorification of God. This does not mean that the gift of interpretation could be overlooked. It is indeed very important.

The Bible specifically made reference to **"other languages"** in the Acts of Apostles:

> **"All of them were filled with the Holy Spirit and began to speak other languages, as the Spirit gave them ability" (Acts of Apostles 2:4).**

Another point of argument is that if it were a native Aramaic or Hebrew language, Jesus would not have made mention of **"new languages",** as we can see from the Gospel of Mark:

> **"And these signs will accompany those who believe: by using my name they cast out demons; they will speak new tongues"(Mk 16:17).**

According to St. Paul, speaking in tongues must be accompanied with interpretation. Otherwise, the believer speaking in tongues must be silent **(1 Cor 14:5, 28).** God is not the author of confusion. The spirits of the prophets are subject to the prophets **(1 Cor 14:32).** This means that believers can exercise self-control and thereby maintain orderliness **(1 Cor 14:40).**

Practice differs among Catholic Charismatic fellowship groups. In most cases, believers speak in tongues in praises-and-worship situation without interpreters. The

Holy Spirit moves mightily during praises and worship which proves that the Holy Spirit is actually in control. St. Paul was so concerned with the fact the public might not understand tongues and so it should not be used without interpretation.

The purpose of the gift of the new language, is praising God! As such, it fulfils its purpose! It is the Holy Spirit that motivates speaking in tongues for the glorification of God. So, failure on the part of believers to understand it does not nullify the purpose of it. Praising God is a sacrifice. As such, **"tongues"** edifies public worship! Biblical reference from the Letter to the Hebrews testifies to this:

> **"Through Him, let us offer God an unending sacrifice of praise, a verbal sacrifice that is offered every time we acknowledge His name"(Heb 13:15).**

Our God is a just God. Those who are offering the fruits of their lips ought to be blessed! "If there is no interpreter present, they must keep quiet in the church and speak only to themselves and to God." **(1 Cor 14:28 "The Jerusalem Bible")** This is St. Paul's governing rule for the **"Gift of Tongues"** which is being violated by some Charismatic Fellowships: some members pray in tongues in praises-and-worship activities, without necessarily having interpretation.

The practice today

From the two references above, it shows that these commands of St. Paul have not been obeyed! Women are being permitted, not only to speak in churches, but are holding strategic positions in churches! Believers speak in tongues, without interpreters in praises-and-worship situations in churches in almost all denominations. Now let us look at St. Paul's command here:

> **"Anyone who claims to be a prophet or inspired ought to recognise that what I am writing to you is a command from the Lord. Unless he recognises this, you should not recognise him" (1 Cor 14:37).**

Judging from the tone of St. Paul's language here, one could say, it is true that he has the authority of the Lord! What can we say about these things? If God is for us, who can be against us? (Rom 8:31).

> **"Prophets can always control their prophetic spirits, since God is not a God of disorder but of peace"(1 Cor 14:32-33).**

Has St. Paul used his expression or authority of the Lord, in a higher sense of spirituality?

Our parish priest, Rev. Fr. Con Boyle, said that if an everyday word is used in a higher sense, it might affect the way we understand it in the ordinary everyday language. So, one could say that it is the case in this situation. So one could conclude here that all St. Paul's hard rules or teachings are summed up in the last sentence of his conclusion:

> **"... but let everything be done with propriety and in order"(1 Cor 14:40).**

The amazing thing about the Spiritual Gifts

The most amazing thing about the spiritual gifts is that every believer has got one, two or more gifts endowed in their lives. Blessed John Henry Newman's quotation about individual **"Service to God"** is important here:

> **"God has created me to do Him some definite service. He has committed some work to me which He has not committed to another. I have my mission. I am a link in a chain, a bond of connection between persons. I shall do good and be a preacher of truth in my place"**
>
> **(For more information www.catholicnews.org.uk)**

This means that every believer has a gift, which when discovered could be used for God's glory. This is exactly what St. Paul is saying in **1 Cor 12:7,** that the spiritual gifts are pooled together for the service and glorification of God – "To each is given the manifestation of the Spirit for the common good".

These gifts are normally dormant in the life of each believer or the faithful. This is because it is difficult to discover it in one's own life. For individual personal spiritual gifts to manifest, that person must satisfy God's prescribed requirements for them:

Faith – without it, it is impossible to please God **(Heb 11: 6)**; Be open to the Holy Spirit – be filled with the desire to receive the gifts;

Conscientiously seek the gifts – "You will seek Me and find Me when you seek with all your heart **(Jer 29:13; Mt 7:7)**. It is good to be aware that the spiritual gift one is asking for will be for God's glory. At the same time individually one would be blessed and edified.

CHAPTER SIX

The symbols of the Holy Spirit

Water – signifies the Holy Spirit's action in Baptism – we were all baptized by one Spirit and drank one Spirit **(1 Cor 12:13)**. As such, the Spirit is also personally the living water welling up from Christ crucified **(Jn 19:34; 1 Jn 5:8)**, as its source and welling up to eternal life **(Jn 4:10-14; Jn 7:38; Exodus 17:1-6; Is 55:1; Zech 14:8; 1 Cor 10:4; Rev 21:6; Rev 22:17)**. Baptism in the Holy Spirit as set out in this text (that is as a renewal of spiritual gifts) cannot be said to be **'essential'** to salvation. It is the Christian Baptism that is essential to salvation, that is, the Baptism commanded by Jesus.

Oil – signifies the Holy Spirit anointing **(1 Jn 2:20, 27; 2 Cor 1:21)**. In RCIA, anointing is the sacramental sign of Confirmation, called "chrismation" in the Eastern Churches. Christ (in Hebrew, Messiah) is the one **"anointed"** by God's Spirit. Jesus is the Anointed (Messiah), the Saviour. Jesus is the one who anoints – as in the wording of the holy chrism anointing, immediately following upon the water part of sacramental Baptism and Confirmation.

Fire – symbolizes the transforming energy of the Holy Spirit's actions. In the form of tongues **"as of fire",** the Holy Spirit rested on the people of God on the Pentecost day and filled them with Himself.

Cloud and light – the Lord God went before His people by day in the pillar of cloud, to lead the way; and by night a pillar of fire, to give them light; to go by day and night **(Exo 13:21)**. The Holy Spirit comes upon the Virgin Mary and "overshadows" her, so that she might conceive and give birth to Jesus. On Mount Tabor, the Mountain of Transfiguration, the Spirit in the "cloud came and overshadowed" Jesus, Moses and Elijah, Peter, James and John, and a "voice came out of the cloud, saying, "This is my Son, my Chosen; listen to Him!" **(Lk 9:34-35)**.

The seal – is a symbol similar to that of anointing. "The Father has set His seal" on Christ and also seals us in Him, **(Jn 6:27; cf. 2 Cor 1:22; Eph 1:13; Eph 4:3-6).** This seal leaves an indelible effect of the anointing with the Holy Spirit in the sacraments of Baptism, Confirmation, and Holy Order. The image of the seal (Sphragis) has been used in some theological traditions to express the indelible **"character"** imprinted by these three unrepeatable sacraments.

The hand – this is one of the wonderful actions of the Holy Spirit. He is given by the imposition or, the laying on, of the hands of the priest. It is one of the signs of the Apostolic Succession. This wonderful all-powerful outpouring of the Holy Spirit is called the **"epiclesis"**.

The finger of God (Jesus) (Lk 11:20) – Jesus says, "If I by the finger of God cast out demons, know that the Kingdom of God has come upon you" **(Lk 11:20; Exodus 31:18)** In the New Testament era, a letter from Christ is written with the Holy Spirit:

> **"... clearly you are an epistle (letter) of Christ, ministered by us, written not with ink but by the Spirit of the living God, not on tablets of stone but on tablets of flesh, that is, of the heart" (2 Cor 3:3).**

The dove – this symbol of the Holy Spirit was manifested when Christ comes up from the water of His baptism. The Holy Spirit, in the form of a dove, comes down upon Him and remains with Him **(Mt 3:16).** The Holy Ghost or the Holy Spirit is the Spirit of God. He is the third person of the Trinity, co-equal with God the Father and God the Son.

The Holy Spirit's dealings with humanity start with the creation of the world. His dealings with the Church (the New Testament period) started about 2000 years ago. The Holy Spirit has been there for ages, not necessarily when there are Holy Spirit phenomena or manifestations. Examples are when love was made manifest between two persons, when God's word was spread and the will of God sought in prayer; when the Eucharist was celebrated and Christians ate the flesh and drank the blood of Christ. The action of the Holy Spirit consists in people been baptized, inspired, healed, comforted, taught, led and empowered.

The Holy Spirit has been addressed within the Bible (King James Version) verses as:

Holy Spirit – Psalm **51:11; Lk 11:13; Eph 1:13**
Spirit – **Rom 8: 16**
Spirit of God – Gen **1:2; Exo 31:1; 1 Sam 11:6; Rom 15:19**
Spirit of the Lord – Judges **3:10; Is 11:2; Acts 8:39**
Spirit of Christ - **Rom 8:9** (one could see here the word **"Spirit"** is linked to the **"Spirit of God"** and the **"Spirit of Christ"**. This **"Spirit"** is referred to as: **"the Holy Spirit"**, the Lord, the giver of life, who proceeds from the Father and the Son in the Creed); **1 Pt 1;11 & 12**
Light of Christ – **2 Cor 4:4; Eph 5:13-14; 1 Jn 1:6-7** This section will be made clear by writing out fully these texts about the **"Light of Christ"**:

> **"In their case the god of this world has blinded the minds of the unbelievers, to keep them from seeing the light of the Gospel of the glory of Christ, who is the image of God"** **(2 Cor 4:4).**

> **"...anything exposed by the light will be illuminated and anything illuminated turns to light. That is why it is said:**

"wake up from your sleep, rise from the dead, and Christ will shine on you" (Eph 5:13-14).

"If we say that we have fellowship with him while we are walking in darkness we lie and do not do what is true; but if we walk in the light as He Himself is in the light, we have fellowship with one another and the blood of Jesus His Son cleanses us from all sin" (1 Jn 1:6-7).

Spirit of Truth – **Jn 14:17; Jn 16:13; 1 Jn 4:6**
In light of the above, the Holy Spirit can manifest gifts of many kinds that may enable a person to:
Be called an apostle **(one sent, a missionary),** a pastor, or a holy person;
Consistently open one's home in hospitality;
Discern needs for, and extend, mercy;
Discern needs for, spiritual, physical and mental conditions;
Evangelize **(spread the Good News);**
Exorcise evil spirits from the possessed;
Feel the presence of God, a powerful sensation through the body, or an overwhelming sense of joy;
Have a personal connection to God;
Have visions;
Hear God speak;
Love and forgive supernaturally;

Perform miracles;

Possess special wisdom, reveal knowledge or supernatural faith;

Prophesy;

Raise the dead;

See angels and demons;

Speak in, or interpret, different languages, including glossolalia **(speaking in tongues)** or religious xenoglossia **(speaking in an unlearned language);**

Understand the Bible (Sacred Scripture), Word of God and teach from it;

Use one's life to help others.

Short reflection on the above virtues

Another way to define **"Renewal"** or **"Life in the Spirit"** is ability to grow spiritually in our journey to eternity. The above virtues, in addition to other spiritual gifts mentioned above, need to be practised. After our new births into the spiritual realm, we need to grow spiritually until we reach the stature of Jesus **(Eph 4:13)**. Jesus says, "If my words abide in you and you abide in Me, ask whatever you want and it will be yours" **(Jn 15:7, 9)**. Grace makes perfect! The power to raise the dead is one of those powers Jesus gave believers, **(Mt 10:7-8; Lk 10:6)**, when He asked them to go out in His name. This power to raise the dead to life is seldomly practised today. It is not practised, because, we are afraid – lack of faith! As long as Jesus is alive, miracles in His name do happen, even today!

CHAPTER SEVEN

The Fruits of the Spirit

The **"Fruits of the Spirit"** are not spiritual gifts, that is to say, that they are not charisms or charismatic gifts. They are manifestations of the virtuous deeds or acts produced by the Holy Spirit in believers. Spiritual gifts are charisms or charismatic gifts **(1 Cor 12:8-10)**. Although, they are given by the influence of the same Spirit, indeed, they serve different functions. We must also remember that the fruits are gratuitous and therefore they are gifts too.

St. Paul gives the fruits of the Spirit in contrast to the works of the flesh **(Gal 5:19)**. So, as the corrupt or sinful nature produces the works of the flesh, so the grace of the Holy Spirit produces the fruits of the Spirit. Just like the fruit of a tree comes from its root, the fruits of the Spirit come from the love of the Spirit, the Third Person of the Blessed Trinity, who is love Himself. He is the love between the Father and the Son.

Here are a few examples of the fruits of the Spirit: It is said that **"True love counts no error" (1 Cor 13:7)**. The virtuous act that enables one to count no error comes from the influence or grace of the Spirit, and so it is the fruit of the Spirit. The fruit of our belief in Christ is to see the glory of God, Jesus tells Martha **(Jn 11:40)**. The fulfilment of a plan or an intention is the fruit of that plan. God's Divine Plan for our salvation is the fruit of the womb of Our Lady, i.e. Our Lord Jesus Christ – the Seed of a woman declared or predicted in **Gen 3:15.**

 Here are a few examples of the fruits of the Spirit contrasted with that of the spiritual or charismatic gifts just to make things clear below:
The power to love God and our neighbour for God's sake is within the domain of the fruits of the Holy Spirit. The power to raise the dead to life is within the domain of the spiritual gifts or charisms. To be at peace with God and our neighbour is a fruit of the Spirit. The healing power to heal diseases is a spiritual or charismatic gift. To cast out demons is a charismatic gift. To have joy in one's life is a fruit of the Spirit. To prophesy is a charismatic gift.

 A further example of the fruits of the Spirit is the ability to turn **"the other cheek" (Mt 5:39).** Interpretations or opinion differ on what **"turn the other cheek"** means. Does Jesus literally mean what He says to His followers **"Turn the other Cheek"?** I will come back to it later.

The 9 fruits of the Spirit
The 9 Fruits of the Spirit according to the Letter to the Galatians, are: Love **(Gk:agape),** Joy, peace, patience, kindness, goodness, faithfulness, gentleness, and self-control **(Gal 5:22-23).**
 In the Catechism of the Catholic Church **(CCC),** there are 12 Fruits of the Holy Spirit: charity, joy, peace, patience,

kindness, goodness, generosity, gentleness, faithfulness, modesty, self-control, and chastity **(CCC 1832 p.170).**

The 8 Spiritual or Charismatic Gifts

Utterance of wisdom, utterance of knowledge, faith, gift of healing, working of miracles, prophecy, discernment of spirits, various kinds of tongues, and interpretation of tongues **(1 Cor 12:8-10).**

Reflection

Faith appears in both the list of the fruits of the Spirit and that of the charismatic gifts. This is because **faith** is common to them both. **Faith** is the basis of anything we can receive from God. Without **faith,** it is impossible to please God **(Heb 11:6).**

The fruits of the Spirit are the base-ground for the charisms, the charismatic gifts. Anyone that does not bear fruits cannot have the charisms. This point can be made clear from the words of Jesus Himself from John's Gospel:

> **"You did not choose Me but I chose you. And I appointed you to go and bear fruit, fruit that will last, so that the Father will give you whatever you ask Him in my name"(Jn 15:16).**

The fruits of the Spirit are even the base-ground for being a disciple of Jesus:

> **"My Father is glorified by this, that you bear much fruit and become my disciples".(Jn 15:8)**

As stated above, I want to give more explanations of the concept of **turning the other cheek: "Turn the Other Cheek"(Mt 5:39)**

"Turn the Other Cheek" is one of the three extraordinary statements Jesus made in His teaching in the **"Sermon on the Mount" (Mt 5:38-41).**
Does Jesus mean this extraordinary message to be applied literally? The answer is **"Yes!"**

Reflection
It is a message of non-retaliation! Let us have a look at Jesus' story when He was being arrested. This story is carried by all the Evangelists in the Bible **(Matthew, Luke, Mark and John).** I want to reflect on that of Matthew and John.

In Matthew's story it reads: "Suddenly, one of those with Jesus put his hand on his sword, and drew it and struck the slave of the high priest, cutting off his ear. Then Jesus said to him,

91

"Put up your sword into its place; for all who take the sword will perish by the sword. "Or do you think that I cannot now appeal to My Father, and He will at once send Me more than 12 legions of angels? "How then could the Scriptures be fulfilled, that it must happen thus?" (Mt 26:51-54).

John's story:

"Simon Peter, who carried a sword, drew it and wounded the high priest's servant, cutting off his right ear. The servant's name was Malchus. Jesus said to Peter, 'put your sword back in its scabbard; am I not to drink the cup that the Father has given me?" (Jn 18:10-11).

Reasons for non-retaliation

From the above two references Jesus gives two vital reasons for non-retaliation:

"For all they that take the sword shall perish with the sword".

Jesus is saying here that the kingdom of God **(the reign of God)** which He brought down from heaven is not retributive law. Jesus says, I have not come to abolish the Law but to fulfil it. **"Turn the Other Check"** is the mandate for fulfilment of the old Retributive Law "an eye for an eye"... **(Mt 5:38-39).** Jesus is the Prince of Peace **(Is 9:6).** He came to administer justice on earth and life in abundance **(Jn 10:10).** Jesus is still telling all Christians today: **"Put your swords into the sheath".** Jesus is also saying:

> **"For our struggle is not against enemies of blood and flesh, but against the rulers, against the authorities, against the cosmic powers of this present darkness, against the spiritual forces of evil in the heavenly places. Therefore take up the whole armour of God, so that you may be able to withstand on that evil day, having done everything, to stand firm. Stand therefore, and fasten the belt of truth around your waist, and put on the breast-plate of righteousness" (Eph 6:12-14).**

Other reasons: Jesus does not give us any tasks without giving us the grace, or supernatural grace and the Holy Spirit commensurate with the task. He made it clear to us in John's Gospel that without Him we can do nothing **(Jn 15:5).** But with God's power within us, nothing shall be impossible to us **(Mt 17:20).**

God's promise to repay for any injustice His people would suffer: Jesus does not want to encourage evil by saying **"Turn the Other Cheek" (Mt 5:39),** but saying

93

"vengeance is Mine", as one can see from the following references from the Bible:

> **"Vengeance is Mine, and recompense; their foot shall slip in due time; For the day of their calamity is at hand, And the things to come hasten upon them" (Deut 32:35); It is said that "God is the Refuge of the Righteous". "O Lord God to whom vengeance belongs – O God, to whom vengeance belongs, shine forth!" Rise up O Judge of the earth. Render punishment to the proud" (Ps 94:1).**

> **Behold, do not avenge yourselves, but rather give place to wrath; for it is written, "Vengeance is Mine, I will repay," says the Lord.**

> **Therefore**
> **"If your enemy is hungry, feed him,**
> **If he is thirsty, give him a drink;**
> **For in so doing you will heap**
> **Coals of fire on his head"(Rom 12:19-20)**

"Turn the Other Cheek" is a command and a glory in disguise! Jesus says "If anyone desires to come after Me, let him deny himself, and take up the cross and follow Me. For whoever desires to save his life will lose it, but whoever loses his life for My sake will find it" **(Mt 16:24-25)**. He who has My commandments and keeps them, it is he who loves Me. And he who loves Me will be loved by My Father, and I will love him and manifest Myself to him" **(Jn 14:21)**. Jesus' commandments mean life!

Reflection

Both the extracts from Matthew's Gospel and John's Gospel show that those who keep His commandments are the ones who actually love Him. Let us examine a phrase from Matthew's Gospel: **"anyone who desires to come after Me, let him deny himself" (Mt 16:24).** Come after Jesus, means coming after the Kingdom of God **(the reign of God).** Coming after the Kingdom of God indeed means the denial of one's life, losing one's honour, respect, dignity and pride for the sake of the Kingdom. The Kingdom of God is taken by violence **(Mt 11:12).** Jesus is the way, the truth and the life **(Jn 14:6).** These Jesus principles are the principles that lead to eternity, that is, to the Father. It is when a seed dies that it produces a new life, the life of the Kingdom, eternity **(Jn 12:44).**

Another pertinent phrase from the Gospel of John is **"He who has My commandments and keeps them ... I will love him and manifest Myself to him".** Jesus manifesting His life to anyone, means that that person will be like Jesus, a true follower of Jesus, who can do what Jesus does **(Jn 14:12).** Jesus manifesting Himself to anyone means that Jesus lives in that person **(Jn 14:23)**. **"For in Him dwells all the fullness of the Godhead bodily and you are complete in Him, who is the head of all principality and power (Col 2:9-10).**

"Turn the Other Cheek" is a symbol of Jesus' sacrificing and freely accepting death for the sake of the Kingdom **(Phil 2:5-8).** The Catholic Church describes Jesus' free acceptance of the death on the cross as the Paschal Mystery — His Passion, Death, Resurrection, and Ascension. Now, anyone reading this little book on **"Renewal of Life"** or **"Life in the Spirit"** or **"baptism of the Holy Spirit"** life will know that the virtuous power to **"turn the other cheek"** is the evidence of the **"Fruits of the Holy Spirit"** in a person. With the action of the Holy Spirit, **"Turn the Other Cheek"** is easy and can be literally carried out! It is a command of Jesus and His commandments are not burdensome or grievous! **(1 Jn 5:3).**

The answers given to the statement **"Turn the Other Cheek",** also equally apply to the remaining two statements:

>**"If anyone wants to sue you and take away your tunic, let him have your cloak also" (Mt 5:40).**

"And whoever compels you to go one mile, go with him two (Mt 5:41).

CHAPTER EIGHT

CONCLUSION
The benefits of the Catholic Charismatic Renewal

It has been said above that renewal is essentially about spiritual growth through the empowerment or boldness of spiritual gifts. The benefits of spiritual gifts are reflected in the following:

Efficiency in Church ministry – participants become more enthusiastic and more zeal is created; zeal for evangelization; deeper love for the Eucharist and Mary Our Mother, more enthusiasm in community living; ecumenical relations **(in the sense used here, it is the ability to relate to non-Catholic Christians).**

Love for Sacred Scripture (the Word of God – the Bible)

There is a beautiful commentary on **Isaiah 55:10-11,** in the first Reading of the First Sunday of Lent by Don Schwager 2015 on the transforming power of the Sacred Scriptures in us which I would like to quote here:

> **"God's word has power to penetrate our dry barren hearts and make them springs of new life. If we let God's word take root in our hearts, it will transform us into the likeness of God Himself and empower us to walk in His way of love and holiness. God's word to guide and shape the way we think, and pray".**

97

Another interesting thing about Scripture is about the poem quoted below from the Divine Office Book I:

"In the Scriptures, by the Spirit, May we see the Saviour's face, Hear His word heed His calling, Know His will and grow in grace".
(Divine Office: Week I Tuesday p.63)

The highest thing to know about renewal is that it is the living of the life of grace, the life of Christ and a holy living – having a continuous relationship with God through Jesus Christ, the only begotten Son, a life of regeneration and transformation **(Rom 12:2; Titus 3:5).** This is what is known as **"Renewal"!** Pope John Paul II calls it **"Life of Grace",**

"True joy, real greatness and supreme dignity can only be found in the life of grace". In the Catholic Charismatic, it is known as "the Life in the Spirit" or "the baptism in the Spirit"
(Gal 5:16; Jn 1:33 "Pope John Paul II")